A Trip
to the Ocean

Written By
Dr. John Morris

Illustrated by
Jonathan Chong

A Trip to the Ocean

First Printing, April 2000

Copyright © 2000 John D. Morris
Interior & Cover Illustrations by Jonathan Chong
Interior Design by Brent Spurlock
Cover Design by Janell Robertson
Edited by Don Goodman

ISBN: 0-89051-285-X
Library of Congress: 99-069309

For information write: **Master Books**
P.O. Box 726
Green Forest, AR 72638

Visit our web site for other great titles: **www.masterbooks.net**

For information regarding publicity contact Dianna Fletcher at 870-438-5288.

Printed in the United States of America

Master
Books

Dedications

This book is dedicated to my youngest daughter, Beth Anna. Her name comes from words used in the Bible, and means "home of grace." Her mother and I pray that her life would always display God's grace within.

John Morris

Dedicated to my two daughters, Jasmine and Jacinthe.

Jonathan Chong

Hi, boys and girls, and welcome to the Institute for Creation Research.

Do you know who works here? Scientists. Scientists who love God. They study all the things God has created.

My name is Tracker John, and I'm a scientist who studies creation, too. I believe that God created the heavens and the earth, just as the Bible says. Knowing that helps me better appreciate the world and all its creatures.

The Institute for Creation Research is in San Diego, California, near the Pacific Ocean. Creation scientists like the ocean because they can see so much of God's handiwork all in one place.

We're about to take a field trip to the ocean. The tide is low today, so we'll see things that are usually underwater. My little dinosaur friend, D. J. (short for Dino Junior), will also come along too.

Climbing down to the shore, we noticed little pools of water. The night before, the sand here was underwater. Now, with the tide out, it was dry except for the water caught in jagged hollows among the rocks. These are called tidepools.

Before we looked around, I gathered my field trip kids together. "Be sure to handle all the sea creatures gently," I told them. "And then return them to their homes. That gives other people a chance to enjoy this part of God's creation, too."

Inside one of the tidepools, Jeremy found a starfish, which is really not a fish at all. It's an animal, also called a sea star, so named for its five arms shaped like a star. Unlike most animals, if it loses an arm, it can grow a new one.

Todd found a sea animal called a sponge. The sponges we use for cleaning at home are copies of the ones God made to live in the ocean.

Beth found a large slug, called
a sea hare. It takes its name from
the two tentacles on its head that make
it look a little like a rabbit. Actually, these
tentacles are not its ears, but its nose. The
sea hare, when threatened by an enemy, hides
itself by squirting a purple
cloud into the water.

"Why does the ocean sometimes rise
up to the cliff, but sometimes it's lower, like it is now?" asked Jeremy.

"That high and low movement
of the ocean," I replied,
"is called the tide."

"What makes the tide?"
asked Beth.

7

Mostly, it's the moon's gravity," I replied. "You know what gravity is, right?" The kids looked puzzled. "Gravity is an unseen force inside everything. It's the earth's gravity that holds you and me and everything else on the ground. It's the sun's gravity that holds the earth in orbit. It's the earth's gravity that holds the moon. And mostly the moon's gravity that makes the tides."

"How does it do that?" asked Beth.

"Imagine a blue tablecloth. Now, in your mind, take hold of it in the middle and lift it a few feet off the table. What happens? The edges move in. And that is what it's like when the moon pulls on the water. Since water moves easily, when the moon's gravity is the strongest over the middle of the ocean, gravity can pick up the water like a tablecloth and the oceans move back from the shores. That's called low tide. When the moon is right over the coast, the water stays high along the shore. High tide."

"What makes the waves?" asked Beth.

"Wind makes the waves. You can see how that works by blowing across the top of the water." Todd blew on the water in a tidepool, sending ripples across the surface.

"Why did God make the tides and the waves?" asked Beth.

"With the seas always in motion, the water stays fresh and carries food to various places. The wind whips the water into waves that nourish the creatures that live near the surface, while the tides bring water to plants and creatures that live near the shores."

The Bible tells us that on the fifth day of Creation, God filled the oceans with an immense variety of plants and animals.

Today, scientists find millions of them living in the water. Some are so small you can see them only under a microscope. And some are gigantic, like the whale shark, the world's largest fish.

God made plants mostly for food. Plants take energy from the sun and get minerals from the water. The energy and the nutrients then pass on to the animals that eat them.

Plants are the first link in what scientists call the food chain.

Small animals eat small plants.
Medium-sized animals eat small animals.
Large animals eat medium-sized animals.
Huge animals eat large animals.

Most people, and certain animals, eat meat and plants.
Whatever the diet, the energy comes from plants.

Plants serve another purpose in God's world," I told my fieldtrippers. "Plants provide fuel. You see, ocean algae was buried by the flood that covered the earth in Noah's day. These buried plants eventually turned into oil, which we use for fuel in vehicles, like cars and planes."

"I have a question," said Beth. "I saw seashells in Oklahoma. How can that be? There's no ocean in Oklahoma."

"Ah, but there was, long ago. The Bible tells us that when God sent the great flood, water covered the entire surface of the earth. It left layers of mud everywhere, including what is now Oklahoma.

In fact, the seashells you saw there help to show that the Flood wasn't just a story. It really happened."

Another one of God's marine wonders is the coral reef. It consists of a colony of smaller animals with stony skeletons. They're often held together by algae.

God created these creatures to help the environment. Coral reefs serve a double purpose. First, they soften the force of waves against a shoreline. Second, and perhaps the most important, they provide an environment in which many animals, including fish, thrive.

Snorkeling, we find another of God's many wonders. This pair of fish enjoys a special relationship. Although the larger fish feeds on smaller fish, it never eats this smaller one swimming alongside. Like a servant, the smaller fish cleans the teeth and the scales of the larger fish. And the larger in turn protects the smaller. Each needs the other to survive.

You know, it's difficult to understand, but some scientists don't believe that God is our Creator. They believe that everything, including plants and animals and people, somehow just got here by a process called evolution. But, we can see, just by looking around, that living things all need each other. Life is so wonderfully balanced. It couldn't just happen.

In our own bodies, all of our organs and all of our systems depend on one another. They had to exist together from the beginning or they wouldn't be here now. That's only one of many proofs that God created everything, just as the Bible says.

According to certain evolution scientists, life began in a place not like any which we can see today. They want us to believe that tiny creatures turned into bigger creatures as if jellyfish turned into lizards that climbed onto shore and turned into birds that turned into countless other creatures that finally turned into men. All this supposedly happened over millions of years.

For me, that's hard to follow and even harder to swallow. These kinds of changes just don't happen. When things change, they don't get better, they get worse.. And let's face it, no creature knows what it needs to become something else.

Let me say this again. One animal cannot become another. God designed it that way. That's what the Bible means when it says God created all creatures after their own kind. When God created mice, their children years and years later were still mice. They didn't turn into human beings. God made the first man and named him Adam.

We raced aboard a scientific research boat where we learned that God made many colorful and amazing ocean creatures. It would take years and years to discover them all!

The boat's operator explained that when a special "scooper" is lowered by rope into the deep ocean, wonderful sea life can be brought to the surface. Glow-in-the-dark fish, squid, and oysters (with beautiful pearls inside!) can be studied this way.

Far out in the ocean, the water is so deep that scientists must make new submarines and underwater cameras to find many creatures.

"In the Bible we are told that God made the ocean to swarm with life," I reminded the children. "Now that we can study all parts of the ocean we see that the Bible is exactly right."

As we gazed at the ocean beyond the coral reefs, I remembered a famous man named Matthew Maury. "He lived in the 1800s," I told the kids. "On his ocean voyages, sailing in certain directions, Maury observed that the water seemed to push against his ship. But sailing in other directions, the water seemed almost to push the ship forward. What, he wondered, was this mysterious force?

"Matthew Maury was an oceanographer, a scientist who studied the ocean. He was also a Christian. Some say he began his search for this mysterious force after reading Psalm 8:8, which tells about the 'paths of the seas.'

"After a long season of close observation, Matthew Maury discovered that these paths were strong underwater currents. He went on to make thorough maps of the ocean's winds and currents. These maps have been used by sailors all over the world. For his work, Matthew Maury earned the title 'Pathfinder of the Seas.' He received honors from many countries."

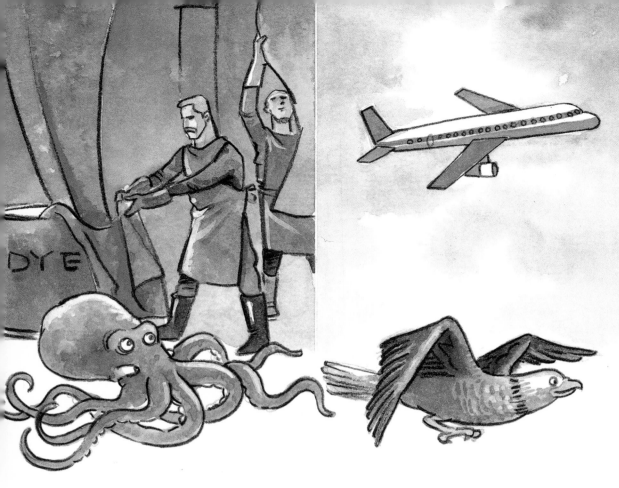

Every day, people discover gifts that God tucked into every corner of His creation. Gifts to make our lives easier or more enjoyable.

- From insects and sea animals, we learn how to produce inks and colored dyes.
- From birds, we design aircraft.
- From plants and animals, we make medicines.
- From bats, we learn radar.
- From our hands, we devise earthmovers.

God's gifts are endless. We need to remind ourselves that we never invent. We merely discover what God built or made possible when He created the world. Our God is an awesome God!

A freighter let us come aboard so we could go farther out to sea. We got there just in time to see a whale burst out of the water. Breathing for the first time in twenty minutes, it shot a geyser of spray from its blowhole. Then it dove into the sea with a booming splash.

"Whales are mammals," I told the kids. "They birth and nurse their babies, just like horses or cats. Except that whales do it underwater."

Beth piped up, "Whales were created on Day Five of Creation Week. It says so right here in Genesis 1:21."

"Yes," I replied, "The Bible also talks about great 'dragons' that lived in the sea."

D.J. quickly moved away from the railing when Tracker John mentioned "dragons!"

"Dragons were real beasts," I explained. "Some of the dragon stories are fairy tales, but others are real. Sailors have seen huge ocean reptiles many times. They told other people what they had seen. Later when people told these stories the memories may have changed into fairy tales, but dragons really existed. Today, we sometimes call them dinosaurs."

Tracker John, did a whale really swallow Jonah?" asked Beth.

"Yes indeed," I replied. "Jesus said it really happened. That's good enough for me. There are some whales and some sharks that are big enough to swallow a man. But, I really think that the fish or whale which swallowed Jonah was especially created by God to do the job."

"God had told Jonah to go to a city called Nineveh and preach, because God wanted the people there to hear about Him. But Jonah disobeyed. He ran off and boarded a ship heading in the opposite direction. God brought a storm against the ship and Jonah ended up inside that huge sea creature, where he finally decided to obey God and go to Nineveh. The huge fish then brought Jonah safely to shore."

We've seen proof that Noah's flood occurred, just as the Bible says. But do you remember God's reason for the flood?"

"Almost everybody was disobeying God," said Beth. "And that made God very angry."

"Right," I told the kids. "The Flood was God's punishment for the peoples' sins. After the Flood, God wanted to start fresh with Noah and his family. They were the only ones who loved God and lived to please Him. But you know, even Noah and his family were sinners. We're all sinners. We all deserve punishment for our sins.

"Thankfully, God promised not to destroy the earth again by flood. He has a new plan. Rather than cleanse the world of sinners, God offers to cleanse the sin from sinners' hearts. To do this, God sent His Son, Jesus, to take our punishment for us."

Who knows how many of Jesus' disciples were fishermen?" I asked.

"At least four," said Beth. "They were Peter, Andrew, James, and John."

"That's right. And Jesus called them away from their jobs, so that He could teach them all they needed to know. 'Come, follow me,' He said, 'and I will make you fishers of men.' Jesus desired for these men to obey Him and serve Him and tell others about Him.

"Jesus desires the same for you and me. 'Come, and follow me,' He asks. But first, we must receive Jesus as our Savior. When He takes away our sins and gives us God's Holy Spirit, we're ready to tell others about Him, so they can come to know Him, too. We can be fishers of men. He will help us.

"Every day I ask for His help in everything I do. I'm a sinner, like everyone else, so I ask Him to help me not to sin. But when I do, I ask Him to forgive me. He loves me, and He forgives me.

"I also ask Jesus to help me in my work as a scientist. I want my work, and everything I do, to please Him. He wants us all to follow Him. That's what I want to do more than anything. Don't you?"

APPENDIX

A. INTERESTING FACTS ABOUT THE OCEAN

- The oceans cover nearly three-fourths of the earth. The water is so deep that all the land could fit inside and still be covered by 10,000 feet of water.

- There are two high tides each day, when the moon is directly overhead or directly on the other side of the earth.

- The two low tides each day occur in between the high tides.

- The highest high tide is called a *spring* tide. It happens when the moon and the sun are pulling in the same direction.

- The lowest low tide is called a *neap* tide. It happens when the sun and the moon are pulling in different directions.

B. INTERESTING ANIMALS IN AND NEAR TIDEPOOLS

LIMPETS: These little mollusks are very common and come in many different shapes. They have one shell covering a "foot" and a "tongue." From the foot comes sticky glue, which holds on to the rock. When the tide rises, they creep around the rock. Their tongue scrapes algae from the rock for a meal.

Some limpets use their tongue to scrape a hole in the rock for their home. They come back to their home in the rock during low tide.

Limpets are either male or female, but some of the males change into females as they grow older.

ABALONES: Larger than limpets, these mollusks eat seaweed. They live in cracks in the rock. Often lots of limpets will be attached to their shell.

Did you ever get a shot of penicillin to fight an infection? Well, penicillin doesn't help with some germs. But abalone blood might. It is used as a medicine to fight some germs. Sometimes the abalone needs help. If it gets cut, the bleeding doesn't stop, and it bleeds to death.

CHITON: (Pronounced K-ton) This little mollusk acts like a roly-poly when scared. When rolled up into a ball, its soft bottom is protected by a hard covering on top.

This hungry creature will eat almost anything. It usually eats algae or seaweed, but sometimes eats small worms or dead animals. Aren't you glad it's not too big?

MUSSELS: Baby mussels attach themselves to a rock and stay there for their whole lives. They make a strong glue which keeps them stuck.

To eat, it opens its shell and uses its tiny hairs to make the water flow through the shell, bringing food.

Lots of people like to eat mussels, but watch out! In the summer time the mussels' food makes them poisonous to humans.

CLAMS: There are many different kinds of clams. They have two shells about the same size. Some burrow in the sand on shore, some stay underwater.

One very interesting clam lives on the ocean bottom, with one end sticking out of the mud. It looks like a little fish is sitting on top, with fins and one eye. It moves just like a fish, too. But this "fish" is really just a part of the clam, and a very important part.

The larvae of this clam must attach themselves to fish until they are older. This fake fish is really just a lure to get fish to come near so that the larvae can take a ride.

SNAILS: These coiled animals come in many shapes and colors. Most crawl along the rocks and eat algae, but others eat mussels or barnacles, using their teeth to open them.

They have eyes on the end of tentacles, which they can pull back in if danger is near. The entire snail can slip back in its shell and protect itself by closing a trap door.

SEA SLUGS: God has created many different creatures, which all look different or have different habits. Some of them have similar features, and have the same general name.

In just that way, there are many kinds of sea slugs, which are really just snails without shells. Their true name is *nudibranch*, which means "naked gill," and reminds us that they have no shell. They look like a garden slug, with a soft body and disgusting feel. Sea slugs come in several colors, red, yellow, orange, brown — some are polka-dotted and some have stripes.

Some eat algae, some eat sea weed, some eat little animals, some eat other sea snails. One type eats sponges, poisonous stickers and all. The slug keeps these stickers in his own body so that if a fish takes a nibble, it spits him right back out.

ANEMONES: These little creatures often look like flowers attached to rocks. They have many tentacles which sway in the moving water. The tentacles may look pretty, but often have stingers, which can sting a passing fish or larvae, providing a meal for the anemone. Certain fish or shrimp, which the anemone doesn't like to eat, like to swim around in the tentacles because they are protected there. Don't worry, though, the stingers may feel sticky, but can't hurt people.

The anemone will shrink back into itself if touched, squirting water out at the same time. If attacked, it has the ability to pinch off a tentacle or two and later grow them back. Sometimes they have a green color. This is due to a colony of tiny plants, which serves the anemone by removing its waste and providing it with oxygen. Remember? This is called symbiosis.

STARFISH: A favorite animal of kids everywhere, this creature doesn't know if it's coming or going, and barely knows if it's right side up or upside down. It has five arms, but no head. It can go in any direction without turning around.

On the bottom of each arm are hundreds of little feet, or suction cups, which hold on tightly to a rock or clam or mussel. The arms and cups are so strong the starfish can pry open a clamshell. To eat the clam is no problem, although our starfish friend doesn't have a mouth. It just sticks its stomach out of the hole on the bottom of the starfish and surrounds the clam. After he has eaten and digested the clam, it brings the stomach back in.

On the starfish's top, it has many soft, fuzzy tufts, through which it breathes. Each clump has tiny pincers in it to keep other animals, like limpets, from hitching a ride. If you hold a starfish's back against your arm, you can feel the pincers gently tugging on your hair when you pull it away.

Many starfish have the ability to grow a new arm, if one gets damaged or broken off.

SEA URCHINS: Often mistaken for a plant, the sea urchin comes in lots of colors and looks like a door knob with nails stuck on it. These sharp spines are used for defense. You'll be sorry if you pick one up the wrong way.

In between the spines are tiny pincers, which keep the larvae of other creatures from living there. Also present are suction feet, which grasp food particles and pass them along to the urchin's mouth, which is on the bottom. Both feet and pincers will grow again if they get knocked off. The main body, called a *test*, is hard and hollow, like an eggshell. A minor crack can heal up, but if it is badly damaged, the animal will die.

Using its feet as pincers, the sea urchin burrows a hole in the rocky shore for protection against the waves. It lives in this burrow as it grows, sometimes getting so big it cannot get out.

BARNACLES: Barnacles look like limpets, but are very different, with legs and shell parts which move. But they don't move around. They find a good spot, like a rock or a ship or even a whale's back, and hang on. They don't have to go get their food. They just sit and wait for food to come to them.

The glue that they produce is one of the strongest natural glues. If you ever try to get one off, you'll understand.

OCTOPUS: These eight-armed creatures are really interesting. Most of us know how they can grow another leg if one gets torn off, and that it can squirt a dark brown ink to escape danger.

But did you know that on each arm are 240 suckers, arranged in double rows? It swims by forcing water out of a nozzle near its head. The squirting water moves the body backward, with the arms trailing along behind.

The octopus has very good vision, with eyes that look very similar to human eyes. It also is quite smart and has been seen to learn lots of things when observed in an aquarium. They are also smart enough to figure out a way to leave most aquariums. Unfortunately, they don't know they can't live on the floor.

Octopi are usually rather small and shy, hiding under rocks or in caves. Some giant ones have been seen with arms up to 100 feet in length.

CRABS: Lots of little crabs can be found along the beach and in tide pools. As scavengers, they will eat almost anything they find. Their hard outer shell gets too small for them as they grow, so they simply get rid of it. Then their skin hardens into another shell.

Hermit crabs live in shells once used by snails. They carry the shell around with them, lay their eggs inside, and escape danger inside.

If a large fish or bird is holding them by a leg or claw, no problem—they can just unhook it and grow another one.

SHRIMP: These little animals are really ugly. They have a hard outer shell and ten legs. They have good vision with two bulging eyes on top of stalks. Their long antennae are equipped with sensitive touch and smell organs. Although they can swim quite well, they prefer to spend their time on the ocean bottom. They will eat almost anything, from seaweed to dead fish to sewage. Maybe that's why they're so ugly. If you find one, watch for quick twitches of movement. Some types have sharp pinchers, which can cut your finger, but those in the tide pools are not so mean. Look at how transparent their bodies are. You can see inside and see its heart beating and the other organs.

C. THE OCEAN'S BIGGEST AND THE SMALLEST AND THE FASTEST AND THE OLDEST

The ocean is truly a strange place. Animals of all shapes and sizes can be found everywhere, even in the deepest part. While most of the animals are normal size, it's fun to think of the really weird ones.

These descriptions were taken mostly from the Guinness Book of World Records.

The Largest Animal: The largest animal is the blue whale. The biggest one ever found was 100 feet long, weighing about 44,000 tons. This is bigger than the biggest dinosaur. He eats nothing but plants.

The Oldest Animal: A sea tortoise lived for 152 years in captivity in France.

The Slowest Growing: A deep sea clam may live for 100 years, but only grows to about one inch long.

The Biggest Egg: A whale shark egg was found which was over 12 inches long. The baby shark inside was almost 14 inches long.

The Heaviest Brain: The sperm whale has a huge head. The biggest ever found had a brain which weighed over 20 pounds.

The Largest Eye: A squid's eye looks very much like a human eye. The largest ever found on a giant squid was 15 inches in diameter.

The Deepest Dive: The sperm whale is quite remarkable. Although no one has ever seen him do it, he probably dives over 2 miles deep in the ocean.

The Longest Living: The maximum life span of a beaked whale is about 70 years.

The Largest Meat Eater: This huge sperm whale eats fish and sharks and anything else. The largest one was 68 feet long.

The Largest Pinniped: (seals, seal lions, and walruses) The southern elephant seal lives near Antarctica. The largest one was 22 feet long and weighted 9,000 pounds.

The Fastest Pinniped: A California sea lion was clocked at 25 miles per hour.

Largest Reptile: The Salt water crocodile in southeast Asia and Australia can grow quite large and eat people. The largest killed was about 27 feet long and weighed over 4000 pounds.

Largest Shark: Sharks are really fish, not mammals like whales. The largest plankton-eating shark measured 61 feet long and weighed 90,000 pounds. The largest meat-eating shark is the great white shark. The largest one on record was 30 feet long weighing 14,000 pounds.

The Longest Fish: An oarfish was seen near New Jersey which was an estimated 50 feet long.

The Heaviest Fish: An ocean sunfish which collided into a boat weighed almost 5,000 pounds. That's a big fish.

The Fastest Fish: It is difficult to measure the speed of fish, but the sailfish, swordfish and merlins are known to be fast. A speed of almost 60 miles an hour was calculated by how far a swordfish stuck into the side of a wooden boat.

The Farthest Flight: Fish don't really fly, but a 'flying' fish was seen to 'fly' over one-half mile.

The Deepest Fish: Believe it or not, a fish was caught at over 5 miles down in the ocean.

The Biggest Starfish: A slender starfish was caught which was 54 inches from tip to tip. The largest regular starfish was 25 inches and weighed 13 pounds.

The Largest Crab: A giant spider crab had a claw span of 12 feet that weighed 41 pounds.

The Largest Lobster: A North Atlantic lobster was 3 feet 6 inches long and weighed 44 pounds.

The Largest Octopus: A skin diver caught an octopus whose arms reached 23 feet and weighed 118 pounds.

The Largest Squid: A monster squid, which ran aground, was 55 feet long and weighed 4,400 pounds.

The Largest Clam: A clam 43 inches across and weighing 580 pounds was found near a coral reef.

The Largest Jellyfish: With tentacles 120 feet long, this jellyfish had a body which was 7 feet 6 inches across.

The Largest Sponge: A huge sponge was collected which was 6 feet around and weighed over 80 pounds.

D. WHAT THE BIBLE SAYS ABOUT THE OCEAN

HOW GOD CREATED THE OCEAN
Gen. 1:9
Gen. 1:20-22
Gen. 1:26
Gen. 1:28
Ps. 8:6-9
Ps. 33:6-8
Ps. 104:24-26
Jer. 31:35
Acts 4:24

THE CREATURES IN THE OCEAN
Job 12:7-10
Lev. 11:46-47
I Cor. 15:39

GOD'S CONTROL OVER THE OCEAN
Ps. 95:3-5
Ecc. 1:7
Matt 8:24-27
Rev. 14:6-7

THE GREAT FLOOD
Gen. 6:17
Gen. 7-10
Gen. 9:11
Gen. 7:20
Ps. 29:3
Ps. 89:9
Ps. 93:3-4

THE OCEAN'S MESSAGE TO US
Deut. 30:10-14
Job 38:16
Ps. 139:7-10
Is. 57:20-21
Micah 7:18-19
Matt. 18:6 B
James 1:5-8
Rev. 5:13
Rev. 21:1

Guide to Subjects in This Book